S0-BOB-580

# EASTER

## Vol. 50, No. 2

**Publisher**, Patricia A. Pingry
**Associate Editor**, Tim Hamling
**Art Director**, Patrick McRae
**Contributing Editors**, Lansing Christman, Deana Deck, Russ Flint, Pamela Kennedy, Heidi King, D. Fran Morley, Nancy J. Skarmeas
**Editorial Asst.**, Donna Sigalos Budjenska

ISBN 0-8249-1107-5

IDEALS—Vol. 50, No. 2 March MCMXCIII IDEALS (ISSN 0019-137X) is published eight times a year: February, March, May, June, August, September, November, December by IDEALS PUBLISHING CORPORATION, P.O. Box 148000, Nashville, Tenn. 37214. Second-class postage paid at Nashville, Tennessee, and additional mailing offices. Copyright © MCMXCII by IDEALS PUBLISHING CORPORATION. POSTMASTER: Send address changes to Ideals, Post Office Box 148000, Nashville, Tenn. 37214-8000. All rights reserved. Title IDEALS registered U.S. Patent Office.

SINGLE ISSUE—$4.95
ONE-YEAR SUBSCRIPTION—eight consecutive issues as published—$19.95
TWO-YEAR SUBSCRIPTION—sixteen consecutive issues as published—$35.95
Outside U.S.A., add $6.00 per subscription year for postage and handling.

### ACKNOWLEDGMENTS

SITTIN' ON THE PORCH by Edgar A. Guest from *WHEN DAY IS DONE*, copyright © 1921 by The Reilly and Lee Co. Used by permission of the author's estate. WHEN DAFFODILS APPEAR from *PASSING CLOUDS* by Patience Strong, copyright © 1959 by Rupert Crew Limited; Our Sincere Thanks to the following authors whom we were unable to contact: Rosaline Guingrich for THE BUTTERFLIES; Edwin Markham for SONG TO A TREE; Georgene Holmes Morton for SPRINGTIME WALK; May Smith White for APRIL'S QUIET HOUR.

Four-color separations by Rayson Films, Inc., Waukesha, Wisconsin.

Printing by The Banta Company, Menasha, Wisconsin. Printed on Weyerhauser Lynx.

The paper used in this publication meets the minimum requirements of American National Standard for Information Sciences—Permanence of Paper for Printed Library Materials, ANSI Z39.48-1984.

Unsolicited manuscripts will not be returned without a self-addressed stamped envelope.

Cover Photo
G. Hampfler/H. Armstrong Roberts

Inside front cover
Frances Hook

Inside back cover
Joseph Maniscalco

# A Light Exists in Spring

Emily Dickinson

A light exists in spring
    Not present on the year
At any other period.
    When March is scarcely here

A color stands abroad
    On solitary hills
That science cannot overtake,
    But human nature feels.

It waits upon the lawn;
    It shows the furthest tree
Upon the furthest slope we know;
    It almost speaks to me.

Then, as horizons step,
    Or noons report away,
Without the formula of sound,
    It passes, and we stay.

A quality of loss
    Affecting our content,
As trade had suddenly encroached
    Upon a sacrament.

Photo Opposite
DAFFODILS
Lancaster, Pennsylvania
Larry Lefever
Grant Heilman Photography

# Spring

Celia Thaxter

The alder by the river
　　Shakes out her powdery curls;
The willow buds in silver
　　For little boys and girls.

The little birds fly over,
　　And, oh, how sweet they sing!
To tell the happy children
　　That once again 'tis spring.

The gay, green grass comes creeping
　　Softly beneath their feet;
The frogs begin to ripple
　　A music clear and sweet.

And buttercups are coming,
　　And scarlet columbine;
And in the sunny meadows
　　The dandelions shine.

And just as many daisies
　　As their soft hands can hold
The little ones may gather,
　　All fair in white and gold.

Here blows the warm, red clover,
　　There peeps the violet blue;
O happy little children,
　　God made them all for you!

Photo Opposite
GREENFIELD GARDENS
Wilmington, North Carolina
Ken Dequaine Photography

# Tapestry of Spring

D. A. Hoover

The dew-wet dawn is radiant, fresh, and still,
The sleepy sun has barely topped the hill;
Light, crisp, and bracing hints of piney breeze
Waft gently from the cones of needled trees.

A blush of pink is restful to the eye;
Between grey trunks, the redbud blossoms fly,
As if afloat like gossamer in flight,
Here, there, with dogwood punctuated white.

The forest floor below, sweet, needle strewn,
Rests in a leafy shade of afternoon.
Bright shafts of sun, like golden arrows too,
The light of tiny blossoms, rich and new.

Small worlds of wonder live as time goes by.
So miniature, they escape the casual eye.
Through many halls the echoing songs of birds,
Sweet, liquid notes of joy, may all be heard.

A place so calm, so natural and fair,
That one may rest his soul while lingering there.

BROOKGREEN GARDENS
Murrells Inlet, South Carolina
William Johnson
Johnson's Photography

# The Butterflies

Rosaline Guingrich

In fragile robes of loveliness
The butterflies invade the world.
Their wings, like sails of flame, unfurled.
They mock the garden with their dress
And pause to return the flowers' caress,

Photo Overleaf
POPPIES, DESERT DANDELION,
DESERT PRIMROSE, AND DAVEY'S GILIA
Poppy Reserve, Antelope Valley, California
Bob Clemenz Photography

TIGER SWALLOWTAIL AND
SPICEBUSH SWALLOWTAIL
Gay Bumgarner, Photographer

And then away—by sunbeams hurled
Into the void of airiness.

And dancing far upon the air,
Surveying the awakening land,
They turn about, a merry band,
And take the garden unaware
And lightly pull the roses' hair.
No merrier vandals one could command
Than those within the garden there.

# Song to a Tree

Edwin Markham

Give me the dance of your boughs, O Tree,
   Whenever the wild wind blows;
And when the wind is gone, give me
   Your beautiful repose.

How easily your greatness swings
   To meet the changing hours;
I, too, would mount upon your wings
   And rest upon your powers.

I seek your grace, O mighty Tree,
   And shall seek, many a day,
Till I more worthily shall be
   Your comrade on the way.

Photo Opposite
RED AND WHITE FLOWERING DOGWOOD
Greenfield Hill, Connecticut
William Johnson
Johnson's Photography

# The Building of the Nest

Margaret Sangster

They'll come again to the apple tree,
    Robin and all the rest,
When the orchard branches are fair to see
    In the snow of the blossom dressed;
And the prettiest thing in the world will be
    The building of the nest.

Weaving it well, so round and trim,
    Hallowing it with care,
Nothing too far away for him,
    Nothing for her too fair,

**14**

Hanging it safe on the topmost limb,
    Their castle in the air.

Ah! mother bird, you'll have weary days
    When the eggs are under your breast,
And shadow may darken the dancing rays
    When the wee ones leave the nest;
But they'll find their wings in a glad amaze,
    And God will see to the rest.

So come to the trees with all your train
    When the apple blossoms blow;
Through the April shimmer of sun and rain,
    Go flying to and fro;
And sing to our hearts as we watch again
    Your fairy building grow.

# Spring's Unfolding Days

Kay Hoffman

Of all the seasons of the year
That call the heart to praise,
There's none I cherish more
Than spring's unfolding days.

A dogwood tree on a hillside near
Bursts forth with blossoms gay;
Bright daffodils are nodding
Where lacy snowflakes lay.

The lawn is sprouting fresh and green,
Bathed with a dewy shine;
Small green leaves are peeping out
From bush and tree and vine.

The robin's morning hymn of praise
'Neath sky of sapphire blue,
The smell of lilacs on rainwashed air
Brings heaven close to you.

I think about His wonders,
How He sends the spring anew;
And in my winter-weary heart,
I find renewal too.

Photo Opposite
PINK DOGWOOD AND AZALEA
Lancaster, Pennsylvania
Larry Lefever
Grant Heilman Photography

HYDRANGEA/Ralph Luedtke

YELLOW ROSE/Ralph Luedtke

## Victory Gardens

Cabbages and carrots parade this month beside roses and orchids at America's great spring flower shows. More than a million paying patrons, thronging for their annual prevue of June, find both the usual feast of color and the new spectacle of kitchen gardens in lush array.

The reason? From Boston to California the shows have become the springboards of the Victory Garden program. From them the nation's eager host of amateur gardeners will aid in helping win the war. "Victory Shows" most of the exhibitions are subtitled, for theirs is a triple service this year—ideas, instruction, and inspiration for you and me. A multitude of men and women with fingers eager to get busy believe that home gardens can serve the country, and the flower shows are leading the way.

Of course, even though Victory Gardens are thus featured, the shows have not forgotten their reason for being, which, in a word, is beauty. It is upon the delight that Americans take in flowers that these mammoth festivals have reared their popularity. A walk through any one of them shows this clearly. Once in a great while you may see a few persons taking notes on some educational display tucked away in a corner. Probably such are knowledgeable gardeners. Everywhere else, with faces rapt, you see the multitude drifting about through the acres of glamorous gardens.

Happily, the marvels the shows create to meet public demand have this year acquired a victory angle as important as that of utilitarian vegetables. Government officials charged with maintaining morale say that opportunities for cultural refreshment are vital these days. They list flowers and gardens high as items of such refreshment. The reasoning is clear when applied to these shows. Enter one of them and, whatever the weather and the news outside, garden after garden reaches away, gay and bright.

Flower shows, of course, go back to the beginning of gardening. In the modern sense they began in England centuries back, when the nobility and the villagers vied in displaying their gardening products. America took up the idea on a large scale only 25 years ago, but since then, mixing business characteristically with beauty, we have made them hum.

Flower shows deserve this popularity for they are the product of the devotion of many enthusiasts whose earnestness is necessary because the big shows are not run to make money. Most are organized as nonprofit corporations. The rest, run by horticultural societies, bear the same relation to their other activities as football does to college athletics. The spring shows, when successful financially, carry other work not self-supporting.

Behind the scenes, each show requires at least a year's planning by a staff of experts, plus months of work by hundreds of other men and women, largely unpaid.

Essentially, the building of a show is the same as the landscaping and planting of some new multi-millionaire's estate. One difference is that the shows are made on acres of dusty floors rather than in friendly soil. Another contrast is that the shows cannot wait upon the season but must beat the calendar by three months.

No prize committee ever pleased all exhibitors, but gardeners who are disappointed find consolation in thinking that next year will be different. They know it will be so for, among the crowds, they see members of the staff show listening to comments and taking notes on faults and merits as well as hints of what the public want most to see.

Indeed, each show has to be different, for there is no standard formula. Like a popular song or a best-selling novel, each show must maintain a balance between novelty and tradition. Only so may the turnstiles keep up their merry clatter and the thousands invested be returned to the sponsors year after year.

Originally printed in *The Christian Science Monitor Magazine*, March 7, 1943.

AGERATUM/Ralph Luedtke

# When Daffodils Appear

Patience Strong

It does something to the heart when daffodils appear,
Dancing gaily underneath the trees.
All the worries and the woes, the sorrow and the fear,
Seem to flutter off upon the breeze.

Something seems to happen to the overburdened heart
When those golden trumpets sound again,
Giving us the wish and will to make another start,
Finding a release from stress and strain.

It's as if God says to us, "Behold, this day I give
The gift of life to every growing thing."
We too, like the daffodils, once more begin to live,
Quickened by the magic of the spring.

Photo Opposite
NATURALIZED DAFFODILS AND
FARMHOUSE
Malvern, Pennsylvania
Jane Grushow
Grant Heilman Photography

# Readers' Reflections

*Editor's note*:
Readers are invited to submit unpublished, original poetry for possible publication in future issues of *Ideals*. Please send copies only; manuscripts will not be returned. Writers receive $10 for each published submission. Send material to "Readers' Reflections," Ideals Publishing Corporation, P.O. Box 140300, Nashville, TN 37214-0300.

## Springtime and Me

I look up through the blossoms
Of peach and apple trees.
Around my feet blue violets
Flutter in the breeze.

I see a bluebird resting
Among pink flowering quince,
A redbird on the wing,
And a robin on the fence.

The lilac bush shows lavender tint,
A soft purple, pastel hue.
Blossoms shaped like fruit of the vine
Are fragrant as heavenly dew.

Earth's smells and sweet fragrances
Brush my face and hair.
I gently touch the blossoms
Light as the billowing air.

Bright azure skies above
Form a blue canopy for green earth.
I know as I look around
That spring has given birth.

Lyla Moore
Nashville, Tennessee

## The Gift of Loving Green

The Lord has sent a gift to me,
A bright and sunny day
With birds on wing that all can see
A-flying on their way.

With flowers green and red around
A-swaying in the air,
They're growing strong
    in garden's ground
With soft and loving care.

The rabbits play among the trees,
So full of life and fun;
God seems so very close to me
When spring comes on the run.

Thank you, Father, for this gift
Of springtime fresh and clean;
It gives my very soul a lift
To see such loving green.

Rev. Stephen MacDonald
Dubuque, Iowa

## Signs of Spring

The air is soft and balmy,
The grass is growing green,
The maple buds are swelling
Till their slender threads are seen

The brown brook chatters gaily
Its rippling course along,
And in the distant tree top,
I hear the bluebird's song.

Madeline Horton
Webster, Massachusetts

## Daffodilly

Little yellow trumpets
Blowing in the wind,
Heralding in springtime
At the winter's end.

Little yellow trumpets
Happy in the sun,
Warm with springtime's sunshine
Now that winter's done.

Little yellow trumpets,
Blowing in the wind,
Songs of heartfelt gladness
For life renewed again.

Leigh Belgique
Salt Lake City, Utah

23

# Springtime Walk

Georgene Holmes Morton

If I should walk beside a brook today,
Where crystal waters ripple soft and low,
And follow its meandering, crooked path,
Some lovely things would charm me, this I know.

For there the creeping grass is velvet green;
The birds pause in a fragrant, cooling breeze.
In feathered, pulsing flight they seek a home
High in the swaying, silvery willow trees.

Gay butterflies, crickets, and moss-green frogs,
So many creatures seek a shelter there;
Embroidered, lacy ferns, violets, wild phlox
Shine in the diamond sunlight, bright and fair.

I argue with my vagrant, gypsy heart:
A shorter way would lead me quickly home;
Some other day I will have leisure time
To leave the hurrying crowd and wide fields roam.

My heart turns a deaf ear to this stern plea
And does not hesitate to disobey;
It knows that I would miss enchanting sights
If I should travel home some other way.

Photo Opposite
FLOWING STREAM AND WATERFALL
Weston, Vermont
Laatsch-Hupp Photography

# A SLICE OF LIFE

Edgar A. Guest

## Sittin' on the Porch

Sittin' on the porch at night when all the tasks
    are done,
Just restin' there an' talkin' with my easy
    slippers on,
An' my shirt band thrown wide open an' my feet
    upon the rail,

Oh, it's then I'm at my richest, with a wealth
    that cannot fail;
For the scent of early roses seems to flood the
    evening air,
An' the throne of downright gladness is my
    wicker rocking chair.

The dog asleep beside me, an' the children rompin' 'round
With their shrieks of merry laughter, Oh, there is no gladder sound
To the ears o' weary mortals, spite of all the scoffers say,
Or a grander bit of music than the children at their play!
An' I tell myself times over, when I'm sittin' there at night,
That the world in which I'm livin' is a place o' real delight.

Then the moon begins its climbin' an' the stars shine overhead,
An' the mother calls the children an' she takes 'em up to bed,
An' I take my pipe in silence an' I think o' many things,
An' balance up my riches with the lonesomeness o' kings,
An' I come to this conclusion, an' I'll wager that I'm right—
That I'm happier than they are, sittin' on my porch at night.

---

*Edgar A. Guest began his illustrious career in 1895 at the age of fourteen when his work first appeared in the* Detroit Free Press. *His column was syndicated in over 300 newspapers, and he became known as "The Poet of the People."*

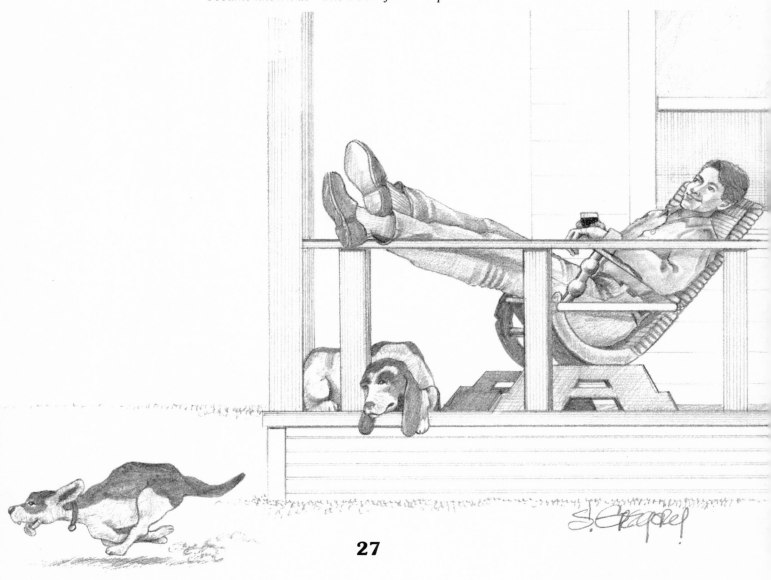

# The Springtime Fairy

Georgia B. Adams

I just saw the springtime fairy,
She was counting daffodils,
She was stirring sleeping tulips,
She was scampering o'er the hills.

She was wafting pretty robins
And provoking their sweet song;
Though the air was still quite chilly,
She assured me not for long.

She was tripping o'er green grasses,
Stooping to the bluebells sweet,
And I wondered what she whispered
As she skipped with dancing feet.

She bid all the clouds be fluffy,
And she painted skies so blue;
I just saw the springtime fairy,
I have seen her, haven't you?

Photo Opposite
TULIPS ALONG FENCEROW
Callaway Gardens, Pine Mountain, Georgia
Laatsch-Hupp Photography

### Ideals'
# Family Recipes

Favorite recipes from the *Ideals'* family of readers

**Editor's note:** If you would like us to consider your favorite recipe, please send a typed copy of the recipe along with your name and address to: *Ideals* Magazine, P.O. Box 140300, Nashville, TN 37214 ATTN: Recipes. We will pay $10 for each recipe used. Recipes cannot be returned.

## HERBED CARROT POTATO SALAD

Boil 6 red potatoes in water until tender. Drain, peel, and cube the potatoes. Peel and grate 1 carrot. Combine carrot and potatoes in a large bowl. Add ¼ cup of thinly sliced celery and 2 tablespoons of pitted black olive slices to the potatoes and sliced carrot.

In a small bowl, combine 2 tablespoons of mayonnaise, 2 tablespoons of plain yogurt, 1 tablespoon of dijon mustard, 1½ teaspoons of snipped chives, 1 teaspoon of lemon juice, 1 teaspoon of Worcestershire sauce, ¼ teaspoon of salt, and ¼ teaspoon of dried dillweed; stir together until well blended. Add dressing to vegetables and toss until vegetables are coated well. Cover and refrigerate for several hours. Serve chilled. Makes 6 servings.

Adria Lauren
Garland, Texas

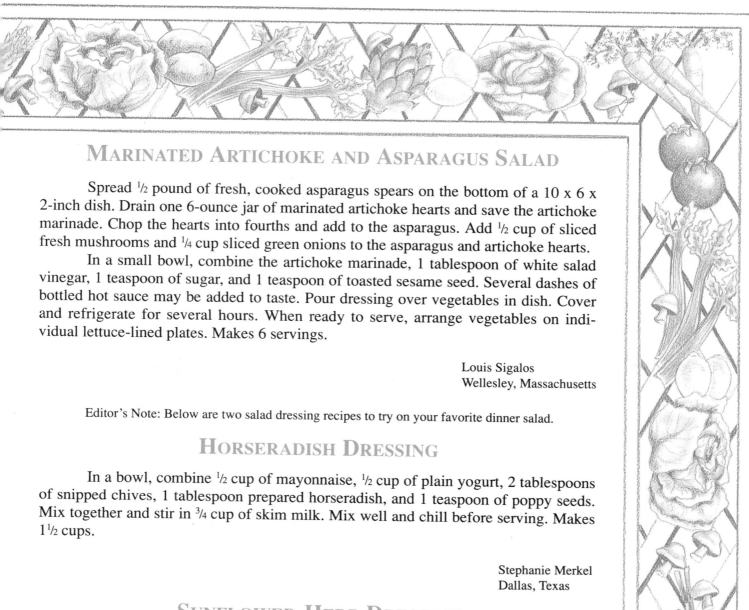

## MARINATED ARTICHOKE AND ASPARAGUS SALAD

Spread ½ pound of fresh, cooked asparagus spears on the bottom of a 10 x 6 x 2-inch dish. Drain one 6-ounce jar of marinated artichoke hearts and save the artichoke marinade. Chop the hearts into fourths and add to the asparagus. Add ½ cup of sliced fresh mushrooms and ¼ cup sliced green onions to the asparagus and artichoke hearts.

In a small bowl, combine the artichoke marinade, 1 tablespoon of white salad vinegar, 1 teaspoon of sugar, and 1 teaspoon of toasted sesame seed. Several dashes of bottled hot sauce may be added to taste. Pour dressing over vegetables in dish. Cover and refrigerate for several hours. When ready to serve, arrange vegetables on individual lettuce-lined plates. Makes 6 servings.

Louis Sigalos
Wellesley, Massachusetts

Editor's Note: Below are two salad dressing recipes to try on your favorite dinner salad.

## HORSERADISH DRESSING

In a bowl, combine ½ cup of mayonnaise, ½ cup of plain yogurt, 2 tablespoons of snipped chives, 1 tablespoon prepared horseradish, and 1 teaspoon of poppy seeds. Mix together and stir in ¾ cup of skim milk. Mix well and chill before serving. Makes 1½ cups.

Stephanie Merkel
Dallas, Texas

## SUNFLOWER-HERB DRESSING

In a blender, combine ¼ cup of unsalted sunflower nuts and 1 clove of minced garlic. Blend together until mixture becomes a very fine powder. Add 1 cup of plain yogurt, 2 tablespoons of skim milk, 1 teaspoon of dried crushed basil, ½ teaspoon of dried crushed thyme, ⅛ teaspoon of dry mustard, and ⅛ teaspoon of pepper. Blend until mixture becomes smooth. Chill before serving. Makes 1 cup.

Paula Saunders
Clifton Forge, Virginia

## FROM MY G·A·R·D·E·N JOURNAL

Deana Deck

Columbine, Colorado state flower, San Isabel National Forest, Colorado, Ed Cooper Photography

## Columbine

The Columbine, stone-blue or deep night brown,
Their honey-comb-like flowers hanging down . . .
John Clare

The Columbine is an ancient garden flower mentioned in documents and literature dating back several centuries; it was included in a poem written in 1310, as well as in works of Chaucer and Shakespeare. Traditionally, its flowers have always been likened to birds. Its botanical name, *Aquilegia canadensis*, derives from the Latin word *aquila*, meaning "eagle." The Saxons called the flower *culfre*, which means "pigeon"; and the common name, columbine, derives from the Latin word *columba*, meaning "dove." The columbine's lovely name appealed to the Italians too. Their word for the flower means "my little dove" in reference to the hanging petals' resemblance to a sleek, long-necked dove bathed in the glow of a Mediterranean sunset.

The unusual, softly colored blossoms of the columbine are long, hollow tubes with delicately flared openings that hang downward from a gently drooping stem. The outer petals surround an inner cup similar to that of the daffodil but much more frail in appearance. The whole assemblage resembles a jester's cap; and, for that reason, the plant has always represented "folly" in the chivalrous language of flowers. James M. Barrie, in one of his whimsical plays, named a sweet but empty-headed character, Columbine.

Wild columbines are very different in color from the many popular garden hybrids; they are uniformly blue and grow in shady woodlands. The modern garden plant, which grows in both sun and partial shade, is available in pink, yellow, red, blue, or purple. My columbines are a rich pink, often bordering on a wine color at the base, and taper to a creamy yellow tinted with pink at the blossom's tip.

The columbine is not difficult to grow. The plant is a perennial that will vigorously self-sow and can be started from seed or root divisions. Since seeds planted in the spring will not produce blooms until the following year, most gardeners purchase one-year-old plants from nurseries. The columbine has a long blooming period, from spring through early summer. It prefers moist, well-drained soil rich in humus and will reach a height of one-and-a-half to two-and-a-half feet. The cut flowers are long lasting in arrangements.

Even when the blooming period has ended, the columbine's flowers do not immediately shrivel and turn brown. Its foliage remains attractive long into fall. Although the columbine is a hardy flower, extra precaution should be taken to protect the plant from the leaf miner, which burrows tunnels in the columbine's leaves. I've been trying to combat them for years, and the best luck I've had so far has been with a combination of systematic insecticide granules worked into the soil in early spring and the use of a light, spun polyester insect barrier.

The columbine has a reputation as a potent medicinal herb that dates back several centuries. It was included in a remedy for the plague in the fourteenth century, was thought to be a cure for the measles and smallpox, and was prescribed with saffron to prevent jaundice. Its roots, when boiled for tea, were thought to remedy fever and scurvy. Seeds, although they are considered poisonous today, were mixed with wine and often prescribed to ease the pain of childbirth.

Even though it has been banished from the medicine chest, the columbine's contribution to pollination makes it a valuable addition to any garden. Hummingbirds are especially attracted to the long-spurred red and yellow petals whose knobbed spurs are filled with nectar. With their long beaks, these energetic birds gain easy access to the sweetness within the bloom. Bees, however, unable to reach within the bloom, often give up in frustration and puncture the knob at the base of the bloom to siphon off the nectar.

Columbine is such a pretty word, such a pretty plant. It's one of my favorites and falls into that category of flowers that you really cannot see the first time you look at it. The iris is the same way, and so are the passionflower and cleome. The columbine's blossom is so gorgeous that it takes your breath away, but it is also so complicated in structure that not until the first rush of infatuation has passed can you ponder its shape and realize how very intricate it is.

---

*Deana Deck lives in Nashville, Tennessee, where her garden column is a regular feature in the* The Tennessean.

# *Handmade Heirloom*

Photo by Robert Schwalb

## Woven Baskets

### Heidi King

Take a quick look around any arts and crafts fair or home decor shop and you are likely to discover an assortment of baskets in unusual shapes, vibrant colors, and a multitude of sizes. One basket may be fashioned into the shape of a watermelon slice, and another may have beads woven in a colorful pattern for a striking finish. With a basket for practically every use and one to match any decorating scheme, it's hard to believe that this ancient craft was originally practiced only for utilitarian purposes.

Historians have traced the art of basketry as far back as the Mesolithic period of the Stone Age. Coiled and plaited work found in the sands of the Nile delta and fragments of basketry and pottery shards found in South America and the Orient prove that many cultures throughout the world simultaneously developed this simple

method of weaving and plaiting.

Early craftsmen added very little decoration or color to the mundane materials used to make their baskets, and each basket was woven with a specific purpose in mind. The earliest baskets were made for carrying, storing, trapping, and harvesting. Later, as the techniques developed, basketry was used in religious rites, funerals, dress, defense, and even as frames in building boats and homes.

In America, the art of basketry evolved from the methods that early European immigrants brought with them from their homelands. They even brought seeds and other raw materials so that they would be able to continue their craft should appropriate fibers not be found. Along with new regional materials, the art of basketry was also heavily influenced by the methods of Native Americans. Additionally, the styles created by the first slaves brought to Georgia and the Carolinas are reflected in the modern basketry of today.

Baskets have been made from a variety of materials, the most common being natural fibers from animals, minerals, or plants indigenous to a particular location. Very often, these fibers are combined into longer strands to add strength. For even more durability, the fibers are sometimes "plied," or twisted, together.

Animal fibers, such as wool, hair, and fur, produce several sizes of yarn that are suitable for basket making. Silk can also be used and is favored over other fibers of the same diameter because of its incredible strength, elasticity, and resilience.

Almost any kind of plant fiber that has a vertical vein can be incorporated into basketry. Most plants are harvested in the spring or fall and will retain their original color if dried in the shade. Before weaving, the materials are soaked in water to increase flexibility. Cotton, linen, sisal, rattan, raffia, and jute are among the more common types of plant fibers used in basketry.

Surprisingly, mineral fibers also contribute to the art of making baskets. Because they are usually expensive, however, minerals are primarily used for decorative purposes. They do not have the elasticity of plant fibers, but their strength lends itself to projects requiring strong frames. Of the earlier forms of basketry, only those used for religious purposes, funerals, and custom dress had any embellishment. When decorations were added, the most popular materials were beads, shells, feathers, and shapes formed from minerals.

From the 1800s through the turn of the century, basket weaving was as much a part of everyday life as quilting, whittling, and other early American crafts. Although the makers of baskets throughout history have predominantly been women, an entire family was usually involved in the production of each basket. The man would gather and cut the materials and hang them to dry—a step that is as time consuming as making the actual basket. The woman would prepare the fibers and shape the frame. Children were taught to weave at an early age and could assist in the final steps. By the time the basket was complete, more than one hundred hours could easily have been spent in the process.

The successful interweaving of materials into baskets is still achieved by hand; it is not yet a mechanized procedure. For this reason, most baskets today are made in countries where labor is inexpensive and the weaving consists of automatic movements with little room for creativity.

Some craftsmen, however, still revel in the slow, intricate work of weaving natural materials into a useful object. Many artisans study traditional basket techniques and then incorporate an individual style into their finished project. It is the combination of techniques passed from one generation to the next and the influences of twentieth-century artists that have made modern basketry a viable art form.

# Little Bits of Spring

Garnett Ann Schultz

A little patch of tulips, all growing bright and fair,
The scent of lovely blossoms perfuming all the air;
A mother robin happy, we hear her gaily sing,
And know that life is glowing with little bits of spring.

The grass is growing greener, the sun is warmer too,
The creek begins to ripple, the sky is turning blue;
So precious are the moments that April days can bring;
And all the world is sparkling with little bits of spring.

Trees that once were lifeless are taking on their green;
The farmer starts his plowing, an ever pleasant scene,
Roller skates and flying kites, so much is happening;
Our hearts are overflowing with little bits of spring.

With little bits of sunshine, an April shower at noon,
The stars a little brighter, a little fuller moon,
God adds his springtime color to every living thing
And glorifies the world with little bits of spring.

Photo Opposite
BLOSSOMING ORCHARDS
Door County, Wisconsin
Ken Dequaine Photography

# COLLECTOR'S CORNER

D. Fran Morley

## Limoges Treasure Boxes

The delicate porcelain treasure boxes prized by collectors for their elegance actually have a very practical history. The boxes, once called *tabatières*, meaning "snuff containers," were originally made for European nobility to hold their daily intake of snuff. Although the glamour of inhaling snuff has certainly faded, the popularity of these "fantasy" boxes has continued to thrive thanks to the fine porcelain being produced in Limoges, France.

For over one hundred years, some of the finest quality porcelains have been manufactured in Limoges, France, about two hundred and fifty miles southwest of Paris. The popularity of

Limoges porcelain, however, owes much to the ancient Orient and the United States. As early as the fourteenth century, European explorers returned from China with beautiful, translucent vases and containers made of materials unknown to Europe. Intrigued by the quality of the imported items, European pottery makers attempted to reproduce them without much success.

The first porcelains produced in Europe were soft-paste porcelains made primarily from refined clay. This process allowed more artistic freedom than the Oriental hard-paste method but was not as durable and not as easy to produce on a large scale. Eventually, scientists determined that a hard clay, kaolin, was necessary to make hard-paste porcelain. When a deposit of kaolin was discovered near Limoges in the middle of the eighteenth century, the wide-scale production of French hard-paste porcelain began.

To be called Limoges, porcelain must have either the Limoges whiteware or decorator mark. Whiteware marks are incised or painted on the piece before the glazing process. Decorator marks are applied over the glaze and serve to identify the company that decorated the piece. Often the decorator and manufacturer are the same, but a piece might be produced in Limoges and painted elsewhere—in Paris or even in the United States.

Limoges porcelain might be a little known, highly exclusive item if not for the work of an American china importer, David Haviland. In 1842, Haviland recognized the economic potential of the area and opened an exporting business in Limoges. Five years later, he added a decorating studio and in 1865, a manufacturing plant. Haviland specialized in elegant porcelain dinner services, but other manufacturers produced more decorative accessories and art objects, such as the porcelain treasure boxes.

These treasure boxes were introduced to the United States by Charles Martine in the early 1950s. He traveled frequently between the two countries to supervise the sculpting and decorating of the pieces. Over the years, the popularity of the boxes has grown enormously. The nearly infinite variety of shapes and designs offer something

Photo Courtesy of S & D Fine Collectibles

for any collector. They are a popular gift item, but one avid collectors would much rather receive than give.

Meticulous care is invested in the production and design of each treasure box. Elegant egg and heart shapes are popular, but other pieces may resemble fruits, vegetables, or animals. Plaster molds made for each individual shape are filled with the hard-paste porcelain and fired in a kiln.

When the Limoges boxes are removed from the kiln, they are all hand painted in beautiful, colorful designs. The inscription *peint main*, meaning "hand painted," and the artist's initials are also added to all authentic Limoges porcelain. Additionally, nearly all of the companies that have manufactured porcelain in the Limoges area for the past century include the words "Limoges" or "France" in their marks for easy identification. These marks help identify the treasure boxes as true Limoges. After the hand painting, the piece is again fired in the kiln to "fix" the colors to the porcelain.

These beautiful, delicate, hand-painted designs are often complemented by equally elegant hand-hammered hinges and clasps. A vegetable-shaped box might have a small, gold bee or fly as a clasp, and a Limoges rabbit may have another small rabbit as its clasp. Such exquisite details explain why these treasure boxes are so valued by Limoges collectors.

# The Glory of the Day

Maxine McCray Miller

Happiness is found in quiet ways,
In sharing common thoughts with kin
    and friends,
In little gifts of smiles throughout our days,
A note or letter that a dear one sends.

Happiness is found in nature's store
Of beauties that surround the countryside:
The peaceful sky, bright mountains,
    fields, and
Oceans with the calling of their tide.

Happiness is found in little things,
A mother's kiss, the clasp of a loved
    one's hand,
In children's laughter, and in birds that sing
In greening trees with their majestic stand.

As dawn is to the glory of the day,
Blessed is the heart that knows the
    happy way.

FLOWERING DOGWOOD AND AZALEAS
Georgetown, South Carolina
Gay Bumgarner, Photographer

# CHRONICLE

Lansing Christman

I watch from the hill as the reds and pinks show so spectacularly the beginning of a new day's sunlight. This Easter dawn—the majestic scene of glory, symbolic of faith, hope, promise, and infinity—is so indicative of the glory of God. The dawn of a new spring rising over the eastern horizon is an enduring and lasting assurance of Christ's resurrection and eternal life. This is a time of reverence and awe, a time of rebirth and renewal.

In the soft whispering winds, so gentle now, I watch the rising sun in a world of blossoming flowers and trees. The fresh, green fields are filled with birdsong. Trees and plants and shrubs wear the various shades of green. This new beginning, as the vernal season renews the world

around us, is filled with the promises of richness, love, and song.

I can sense the very rhythms of the universe, the pulse and heartbeat of life, and know that my faith is made more secure. I sense the softness of the heavens, the magnificence and awe of a warming and reawakening underfoot.

Knowing these things, there is room in my heart for only love and compassion. There is room for only peace and the security of faith. "For God so loved the world, that he gave his only begotten Son, that whosoever believeth in him should not perish, but have everlasting life."

I recall something Clara Sapp Gramling of Gramling, South Carolina, wrote in her recently published book, *Angel in the Tree*, that seems especially appropriate as we celebrate this Easter season:

> Let us be grateful for each heartache that assails us;
> Let us be grateful for each sorrow and care;
> They only tend to make us stronger—
> The load of someone else we learn to share.

*The author of two published books, Lansing Christman has been contributing to* Ideals *for almost twenty years. Mr. Christman has also been published in several American, foreign, and braille anthologies. He lives in rural South Carolina.*

# EASTER DAY

E'Lane Carlisle Murray

As night recedes, the early dawn
Moves lightly on the flowered lawn
And touches people on their way
To celebrate Christ's holy day.

Through stained glass panes of purple hue
Inside each church, the light shines through
On lilies whose white, silken sheen
Is tinged with springtime's softest green.

Above the altar, lifted high,
The empty cross points to the sky,
While joyous voices join and sing
Of Easter and the risen King.

Photo Opposite
WHITE DOGWOOD AND CHURCH
Savannah, Georgia
Gay Bumgarner, Photographer

# BITS & PIECES

Fairer grows the earth each morning
    To the eyes that watch aright;
Every dewdrop sparkles warning
    Of a miracle in sight;
Of some unexpected glory
    Waiting in the old and plain;
Poet's dream nor travel's story
    Works such wonders as remain.

          William C. Gannett

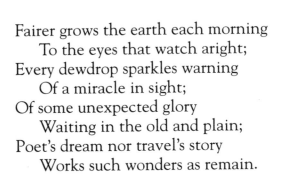

Whoever wakens on a day,
    Happy to know and be,
To enjoy the air, to love his kind,
    To labor, to be free—
Already his enraptured soul
    Lives in eternity.

          Bliss Carman

God illustrates His meaning by the fragments
of light and beauty which are scattered on
the higher side of our own inferior world.
Everywhere, could we but see it, He has set
up a ladder by which we may reach the skies.

          Joseph Parker

Wide flush the fields; the softening air is balm;
echo the mountains round; the forest smiles;
and every sense, and every heart is joy.

James Thomson

In the Spring a livelier iris changes on the
    burnish'd dove;
In the Spring a young man's fancy lightly
    turns to thoughts of love.

Alfred, Lord Tennyson

Stately spring! whose robe-folds are valleys,
whose breast-bouquet is gardens, and whose
blush is a vernal evening.

Jean Paul Richter

O springtime sweet!
Over the hills come thy lovely feet,
The earth's white mantle is cast away,
She clothes herself all in green today;
And the little flowers that hid from the cold
Are springing anew from the warm, fresh mould.

O springtime sweet!
The whole earth smiles thy coming to greet;
Our hearts to their inmost depths are stirred
By the first spring flower and the song of the bird;
Our sweet, strange feelings no room can find,
They wander like dreams through heart and mind.

James Freeman Clarke

**47**

# THE ENTRY INTO JERUSALEM

And when they came nigh
to Jerusalem, unto Bethphage and Bethany, at the
mount of Olives, he sendeth forth two of his disciples,
And saith unto them, Go your way into the village
over against you: and as soon as ye be entered into it,
ye shall find a colt tied, whereon never man sat;
loose him, and bring him. And if any man say unto you,
Why do ye this? say ye that the Lord hath need of him;
and straightway he will send him hither.

And they went their way, and found the colt tied by the door
without in a place where two ways met; and they loose him.
And certain of them that stood there said unto them,
What do ye, loosing the colt? And they said unto them
even as Jesus had commanded: and they let them go.

And they brought the colt to Jesus, and cast their garments
on him; and he sat upon him. And many spread
their garments in the way: and others cut down
branches off the trees, and strawed them in the way.

And they that went before, and they that followed,
cried, saying, Hosanna; Blessed is he that cometh
in the name of the Lord: Blessed be the kingdom
of our father David, that cometh in the name of the Lord:
Hosanna in the highest.
And Jesus entered into Jerusalem, and into the temple. . . .

MARK 11:1-11

Giotto (1267?-1336/7)
THE ENTRY OF CHRIST INTO JERUSALEM, 1305-6
Scrovegni Chapel, Padua, Italy
Scala/Art Resource, New York

# THE LAST SUPPER

*nd when the hour*
*was come, he sat down,*
*and the twelve apostles with him.*
*And he said unto them,*
*With desire I have desired to eat*
*this passover with you before I suffer:*
*For I say unto you,*
*I will not any more eat thereof,*
*until it be fulfilled in the kingdom of God.*

*And he took the cup,*
*and gave thanks, and said,*
*Take this, and divide it among yourselves;*
*For I say unto you,*
*I will not drink of the fruit of the vine,*
*until the kingdom of God shall come.*

*And he took the bread,*
*and gave thanks, and brake it,*
*and gave unto them saying,*
*This is my body which is given for you:*
*this do in remembrance of me.*

*Likewise also the cup after supper, saying,*
*This cup is the new testament in my blood,*
*which is shed for you.*

LUKE 22: 14-20

Giotto (1267?-1336/7)
THE LAST SUPPER, 1305-6
Scrovegni Chapel, Padua, Italy
Scala/Art Resource, New York

# THE BETRAYAL

And while he
yet spake, behold a multitude,
and he that was called Judas,
one of the twelve, went before them,
and drew near unto Jesus to kiss him.

But Jesus said unto him, Judas,
betrayest thou the Son of man with a kiss?
When they which were about him saw
what would follow, they said unto him,
Lord, shall we smite with the sword?
And one of them smote the servant of
the high priest, and cut off his right ear.

And Jesus answered and said,
Suffer ye thus far. And he touched his ear,
and healed him. Then Jesus said unto
the chief priests, and captains of the temple,
and the elders, which were come to him.
Be ye come out, as against a thief,
with swords and staves?
When I was daily with you in the temple,
ye stretched forth no hands against me:
but this is your hour, and the power of darkness.

LUKE 22: 47-53

Giotto (1267?-1336/7)
THE KISS OF JUDAS, 1305-6
Scrovegni Chapel, Padua, Italy
Scala/Art Resource, New York

# THE TRIAL

**A**nd the chief priests
and all the council sought for witness against
Jesus to put him to death; and found none.

And there arose certain,
and bare false witness against him, saying,
We heard him say, I will destroy this temple
that is made with hands, and within three days
I will build another made without hands.

And the high priest stood up in the midst,
and asked Jesus, saying, Answerest thou nothing?
what is it which these witness against thee?
But he held his peace, and answered nothing.
Again the high priest asked him, and said unto him,
Art thou the Christ, the Son of the Blessed?

And Jesus said, I am: and ye shall see
the Son of man sitting on the right hand of power,
and coming in the clouds of heaven.

Then the high priest rent his clothes, and saith,
What need we any further witnesses? Ye have heard
the blasphemy: what think ye? And they all
condemned him to be guilty of death.

MARK 14: 55, 57-58, 60-64

Giotto (1267?-1336/7)
JESUS BEFORE CAIAPHAS, 1305-6
Scrovegni Chapel, Padua, Italy
Scala/Art Resource, New York

# THE CRUCIFIXION

And Pilate answered
and said again unto them, What will ye then
that I shall do unto him whom ye call
the King of the Jews? And they cried out again,
Crucify him. Then Pilate said unto them,
Why, what evil hath he done?
And they cried out the more exceedingly,
Crucify him.

And so Pilate, willing to content the people,
released Barabbas unto them, and delivered Jesus,
when he had scourged him, to be crucified.
And the soldiers led him away
into the hall, called Praetorium;
and they call together the whole band.

And they clothed him with purple,
and platted a crown of thorns,
and put it about his head,
And began to salute him,
Hail, King of the Jews!
And they smote him on the head with a reed,
and did spit upon him,
and bowing their knees worshipped him.
And when they had mocked him,
they took off the purple from him,
and put his own clothes on him,
and led him out to crucify him.

MARK 15: 12-20

Giotto (1267?-1336/7)
THE CRUCIFIXION, 1305-6
Scrovegni Chapel, Padua, Italy
Scala/Art Resource, New York

# THE APPEARANCE

But Mary stood without
at the sepulchre weeping: and as she wept,
she stooped down, and looked into the sepulchre,
And seeth two angels in white sitting,
the one at the head, and the other at the feet,
where the body of Jesus had lain.
And they say unto her, Woman, why weepest thou?
She saith unto them, Because they have taken away my Lord,
and I know not where they have laid him.

And when she had thus said, she turned herself back,
and saw Jesus standing, and knew not that it was Jesus.
Jesus saith unto her,
Woman, why weepest thou? whom seekest thou?
She, supposing him to be the gardener, saith unto him,
Sir, if thou have borne him hence,
tell me where thou hast laid him, and I will take him away.
Jesus saith unto her, Mary.
She turned herself, and saith unto him,
Rabboni; which is to say, Master.

Jesus saith unto her, Touch me not;
for I am not yet ascended to my Father:
but go to my brethren, and say unto them,
I ascend unto my Father, and your Father;
and to my God, and your God.

JOHN 20: 11-17

Giotto (1267?-1336/7)
NOLI ME TANGERE, 1305-6
Scrovegni Chapel, Padua, Italy
Scala/Art Resource, New York

# THE ASCENSION

And he said
unto them, These are the words
which I spake unto you,
while I was yet with you,
that all things must be fulfilled,
which were written in the law of Moses,
and in the prophets, and in the psalms, concerning me.
Then opened he their understanding,
that they might understand the scriptures, And
said unto them, Thus it is written,
and thus it behoved Christ to suffer,
and to rise from the dead the third day:

And ye are witnesses of these things.
And he led them out as far as to Bethany,
and he lifted up his hands, and blessed them.
And it came to pass, while he blessed them,
he was parted from them,
and carried up into heaven.
And they worshipped him,
and returned to Jerusalem with great joy:
And were continually in the temple,
praising and blessing God.
Amen.

Luke 24: 44-46, 48, 50-53

# FOR THE CHILDREN

ARTWORK BY RUSS FLINT

## An Easter Carol

Christina Georgina Rossetti

Spring bursts today,
For Christ is risen and all the earth's at play.
    Flash forth, thou Sun.
The rain is over and gone; its work is done.

Winter is past,
Sweet spring is come at last, is come at last.
    Bud, fig, and vine,
Bud, olive, fat with fruit and oil and wine.

Break forth this morn
In roses, thou but yesterday a thorn.
    Uplift thy head,
O pure white lily through the winter dead.

Beside your dams
Leap and rejoice, you merrymaking lambs.
    All herds and flocks
Rejoice, all beasts of thickets and of rocks.

Sing, creatures, sing,
Angels and men and birds and everything.

# At Easter Time

Laura Elizabeth Richards

The little flowers came through the ground,
    At Easter time, at Easter time;
They raised their heads and looked around
    At happy Easter time.
And every pretty bud did say,
    "Good people, bless this holy day,
For Christ is risen, the angels say,
    At happy Easter time!"

The pure white lily raised its cup
    At Easter time, at Easter time;
The crocus to the sky looked up
    At happy Easter time.
"We'll hear the song of heaven!" they say,
    "Its glory shines on us today.
Oh! may it shine on us always
    At holy Easter time!"

'Twas long and long and long ago,
    That Easter time, that Easter time;
But still the pure white lilies blow
    At happy Easter time.
And still each little flower doth say,
    "Good Christians, bless this holy day,
For Christ is risen, the angels say
    At blessed Easter time!"

# THROUGH MY WINDOW

### Pamela Kennedy

## Guard Duty

"Jason, Marcus, Articus! Come here!"

The orders echoed across the garrison's courtyard as the three soldiers hurried to the centurion's side, stood at attention, and saluted.

"These priests from the temple have requested a guard for the tomb of their recently deceased friend . . ."

"He was most certainly not our friend," interrupted one of the rabbis.

". . . and Pilate has graciously granted this unusual request," the centurion continued. "You three are to make certain that thieves do not break into the tomb. Jason, you lead the guard and remember, you represent Rome. That is all."

"Come along," an aging rabbi ordered, and the small party walked quickly through the garrison's gates and along the dusty streets of Jerusalem until they came to a small walled gar-den. At the garden's far side, shaded by an ancient acacia, was a large tomb, its entrance sealed with a rough stone wheel.

"There it is," announced one of the rabbis. "The body is inside, but we suspect his followers may try to steal it in order to feign a resurrection. It will be your responsibility to see that this does not occur. Do you understand?"

Jason's face flushed with anger at the priest's tone. "I am sure we shall have no difficulty," he replied, "but to ease your minds, we shall place a Roman seal upon the tomb." Apparently satisfied with this extra precaution, the old rabbi and his fellow priests left the soldiers to their task.

Through the night, the guards took their turns on watch. At dawn, Jason stood beside the acacia as a gentle breeze swept through the garden. Suddenly, the wind hushed, the birds became still, and the leaves hung motionless. Jason's pulse began to race, and he dashed to wake the others. "Get up! Hurry! Something very odd is happening."

The earth began to roll and pitch, and the guards staggered, clinging to one another for support. A brilliant light enveloped the garden. Stunned, Articus pointed a trembling finger toward the tomb. "Look!" he gasped.

A man dressed in dazzling white effortlessly pushed the heavy stone away from the tomb's entrance. Then, seating himself upon the stone, he examined the trio of soldiers. Jason's heart pounded and his body shook with terror as he and his fellow guards shrunk beneath the angel's gaze. Overcome with fear, the three fell to the ground, unconscious.

Jason was the first to rise. The blinding light was gone, and he heard muffled voices near the open tomb. Gathering his courage, he slowly edged nearer until he could make out two women conversing with the angel. He held his breath, listening to their words.

The angel comforted them, then said: "Be not affrighted: Ye seek Jesus of Nazareth which was crucified: he is risen; he is not here: behold the place where they laid him. But go your way, tell his disciples and Peter that he goeth before you into Galilee: there shall ye see him, as he said unto you."

The women looked at the angel with awe and then gripped each other in a joyful embrace. "Go now," the angel urged, and the two women hurried from the garden. The angel turned, and his eyes met Jason's for one piercing moment. Then he was gone, vanished; only the dim light of the early dawn remained.

Jason glanced back at his fellow guards, still unconscious on the ground, then crept slowly to the tomb. Stepping over the broken Roman seal, he entered the crypt. Once inside, he saw the linen clothes lying undisturbed on the bier as if the body had merely evaporated from within them. He recalled the mysterious man's words: "He is risen."

Hastening outside again, Jason ran to Articus and Marcus, who were beginning to stir. "The body is gone," he announced. He did not tell them of the women, the angel's words, nor the empty grave clothes; it was all too bewildering.

"How are we going to explain this?" asked Articus angrily. "The centurion will have our heads for this, mark my words."

Jason thought for a moment. "It was the rabbis who insisted upon the guards. I suggest we go to them first. At least we can buy some time."

The three soldiers quickly gathered their gear and ran to the temple's courtyard. Jason asked Articus to speak. Slowly and dramatically, he told the incredulous rabbi of the earthquake, the rolling back of the stone, and the man dressed in glowing white. When Articus finished, the priest instructed the soldiers to wait while he conferred with his fellow rabbis.

Shortly, the chief priest returned. He handed Jason a leather bag. "Here is a very large sum of money. You are to divide it among yourselves and must never reveal its source. If you are questioned about your experiences this morning, you are to say this: 'His disciples came by night, and stole him away while we slept.' And if this come to the governor's ears, we will persuade him, and secure you. Now be off and let me never see any of you again."

As they returned to the garrison, the three divided the Roman coins carefully. Articus and Marcus joked about how they would spend their windfall and turned to Jason, who thoughtfully fingered his coins. "What about you, Jason, what will you buy?" teased Articus.

Testing the weight of the gold, Jason recalled the angel's words, "He is risen!" He remembered the women's joy and their haste to share the news. He regarded his friends for a moment then replied, "I have decided to go to Galilee. There is someone there I need to see."

---

*Pamela Kennedy is a freelance writer of short stories, articles, essays, and children's books. Married to a naval officer and mother of three children, she has made her home on both U.S. coasts and in Hawaii and currently resides in Washington, D.C. She draws her material from her own experiences and memories, adding bits of her imagination to create a story or mood.*

# April's Quiet Hour

May Smith White

Here is the day I long have sought,
Hushed, as when the echo dies.
Now could it be that springtime draws
Her stillness from the April skies?

Last night each lilac bud unfolded—
They chose that time when day is done—
Softly purling each dewy petal
To greet the early morning sun.

Through years, as April comes, I know
That I shall watch each budding flower
And feel again that balm that comes
To those who wait this holy hour.

Photo Opposite
BASKET OF HANGING IMPATIENS
Columbus, Ohio
Adam Jones, Photographer

# TRAVELER'S Diary

Tim Hamling

Main Hall/The Huntington Gallery. Courtesy of the Huntington Library.

## The Huntington and the Gutenberg Bible

In 1919, Henry and Arabella Huntington transferred their estate in San Marino, California, to a non-profit, educational trust that created the Huntington Library, Art Collections, and Botanical Gardens. Although it is composed of three seemingly distinct parts, the Huntington remains unified by its "devotion to research, education, and beauty."

The Huntington Botanical Gardens decorate the rolling lawns of the estate with fifteen specialized gardens and more than fourteen thousand varieties of plants covering over one hundred and fifty acres of the two hundred and seven acre grounds. The Japanese Garden includes bonsai, Japanese cedars, stone lanterns, pagodas, and an authentic Japanese house. The Desert Garden along the eastern boundary of the grounds includes over twenty-five hundred species of desert plants. In the Rose Garden, the variety of species being cultivated enables a visitor to trace the history of the rose more than one thousand years to roses that grew in Medieval Europe.

Equal in variety and beauty to the gardens are the Huntington Art Collections. The former Huntington mansion now houses the Huntington Art Gallery. The interior rooms modeled on French and British rooms of the eighteenth century are the perfect complement to the vast collection of French and British paintings of the eighteenth and nineteenth centuries, including two world-famous, full-length portraits by British painters: Thomas Gainsborough's *Blue Boy* and Thomas Lawrence's *Pinkie*. The Virginia Steele Scott Gallery houses American paintings dating from the 1730s to the 1930s and includes works by John Singleton Copley, Mary Cassatt, Thomas Moran, and Edward Hopper. The Arabella Huntington Memorial Collection, which Henry established in memory of his late wife, contains Renaissance paintings and eighteenth-century French porcelain, sculpture, and furniture and occupies the west wing of the Huntington Library.

This magnificent library houses an impressive collection of rare books and manuscripts devoted to British and American history and literature. From Captain John Smith's early account of Virginia and the American colonies through manuscripts describing the American Revolution, the nation's early struggles are well documented. Letters and journals from settlers on the western frontier, Civil War documents by Abraham Lincoln and Clara Barton, and literature by uniquely American writers, such as Walt Whitman, Mark Twain, Henry Hawthorne, Herman Melville, Henry David Thoreau, and Ralph Waldo Emerson, detail the expansion and hardships facing the nation as it grew to maturity.

The library's holdings of British literature are equally impressive. Included is the early-fifteenth century Ellesmere manuscript of Chaucer's *The Canterbury Tales*, the most complete and reliable, as well as the most elaborately decorated, of any existing version. The Huntington also contains a more comprehensive collection of the early editions of Shakespeare's work than any other library in the world. The library's 1623 edition of the playwright's *Comedies, Histories, and Tragedies*, the legendary "First Folio," is the volume that ensured the preservation of many of Shakespeare's finest plays.

The Huntington Library also contains a copy of the Gutenberg Bible, the first book printed with movable type in Europe. Printed around 1455 by Johannes Gutenberg, the inventor of printing in the western world, the Gutenberg contains the Old and New Testaments and the Apocrypha. The text is in the Latin Vulgate version and arranged in forty-two line columns. Although the text's arrangement is considered to be an uneconomic use of space, the technical efficiency in the Gutenberg's printing was not improved upon until the nineteenth century.

The text, set in type called black-letter or gothic, gives a majestic and medieval feeling to the Gutenberg. Only the text, however, was printed; the chapter headings, initials, and marginal decorations were all added by hand after the printing. The Huntington copy is one of forty-eight surviving copies overall and one of only twelve surviving copies printed on vellum, the inner skin of a calf or sheep. The binding on the Huntington Gutenberg is contemporary with the fifteenth-century printing of the text and consists of stamped calfskin covering heavy oak boards.

Henry Huntington purchased the Bible at an estate sale in New York in 1911. Outbidding some of the wealthiest and most prominent book collectors in the world, Huntington purchased the Gutenberg for $50,000, the highest price ever paid for a book at that time. Although many accused him of overbidding, Huntington's purchase has proved exceedingly shrewd. A recently auctioned Gutenberg Bible sold for several million dollars.

The Huntington Library is a fitting home for the Gutenberg Bible. The meticulous attention and precise technical craft that produced the masterpiece are the same qualities used to preserve all the Huntington's treasures. The Huntingtons' passion for books, fine art, and gardens laid the foundation for one of the nation's finest cultural and educational centers that today attracts scholars and visitors from all over the world.

Detail of the Gutenberg Bible. Courtesy of the Huntington Library.

# The Church in the Valley

Loise Pinkerton Fritz

There's a little white church in the valley,
Nearby where the still waters flow,
And where, in the beauty of springtime,
The colorful wildflowers grow.

A little white church with a steeple
In which hangs a golden-hued bell
That chimes out so sweetly each Sunday,
Echoing all through the dell.

In this little white church in the valley,
There's a special rejoicing today;
For here in the beauty of springtime,
Easter is holding full sway.

Its spirit sets heartstrings to singing
This message of newness and life,
A truth that will keep on blooming
When past is this Eastertide.

Photo Opposite
GRANGE & EPISCOPAL CHURCH
Bridgewater, Connecticut
William Johnson
Johnson's Photography

# LEGENDARY AMERICANS

Nancy Skarmeas

## Henry Huntington

When asked to explain the reasons for his success, Henry Huntington offered a simple answer: always be well prepared and "on the job all the time." The thoroughness with which Huntington adhered to this philosophy is evident in all aspects of his life, from his business achievements to his book and art collections to his philanthropic efforts. Huntington's accomplishments in these three areas continue to be felt today throughout the country.

Born in 1850 in Oneonta, New York, Henry Huntington received his education in the schools of his hometown. He learned the merits of hard work and diligence early through his first job as a clerk in a local hardware store. At age twenty, Huntington accepted a position with a large hardware company in New York City, but he held this job for only one year. In 1871, Henry's uncle, Collis P. Huntington, asked him to leave New York to manage a sawmill in West Virginia.

Collis Huntington was one of the pioneer American railroad builders of the period, and he used the timber from the sawmill for his railway construction. This move began a lifetime involvement in transportation for Huntington, who managed the sawmill for five years and eventually became its owner. He returned to Oneonta for a time before he took a job in 1881 with one of his uncle's railway lines. Huntington became superintendent of a portion of the line's construction that eventually formed part of the Chesapeake, Ohio & Southwestern Railroad.

Like the railroads he managed, Huntington gradually moved west toward his ultimate destination of California. In 1884, he became superintendent of construction on the Kentucky Central Railroad. He occupied various positions with this line before becoming its vice-president and general manager in 1887. During this time, Huntington also served as director of the various railways in which his uncle had an interest. This varied experience in multiple levels of the railroad encouraged Collis Huntington to invite his nephew to San Francisco to join the Southern Pacific Railway.

Henry Huntington moved to California in 1892 and served as a vice-president for Southern Pacific for eight years. During this time, he also became interested in the intra-urban transportation for the city. He improved and expanded San Francisco's system, and in 1898, he began to invest and consolidate the city transportation system in Los Angeles.

When Collis Huntington died in 1900, Henry inherited his immense fortune, but he quickly sold his interests in Southern Pacific Railway and devoted his time to developing an inter-urban transportation network in Southern California. Using his extensive knowledge gained from his years working with the railways, Huntington planned a system that would extend from Santa Barbara to San Diego and from the mountains in the west to the coast in the east. He eventually sold these lines to the Southern Pacific Railway in 1910.

Although he sold his transportation interests, Huntington continued to influence the development of Southern California. He helped promote electrical power and invested wisely in the area's valuable real estate. In 1903, he purchased the San Marino Ranch, which became his residence and home of his splendid collections of British and American fine art and rare books.

Huntington applied the same thoroughness and knowledge he employed in running the railways to acquiring his collections. He purchased entire libraries from other wealthy collectors as well as individual books from estate sales. He did not buy manuscripts randomly; like all aspects of his life, he had a plan and vision for his collections. At his death in 1927, his library was among the best in the country for materials on British literature and among the best in the world for its material on the history of America.

Huntington applied the same devotion to his art collections and his botanical gardens; he employed experts to oversee their care and growth. Although his art collections reveal a preference for British and American artwork, his galleries also included French and Italian Renaissance pieces. The diversity in his botanical gardens is testimony to his appreciation for nature's variety and beauty.

The amount of work invested in the estate and collections convinced Huntington to ensure their preservation following his death. Consequently, in 1919, Henry and his wife, Arabella, signed a deed that transferred the San Marino estate and collections to an educational trust with an endowment that provided for its operation. The Huntingtons' foresight ensured that their estate remained intact for both visitors and scholars hoping to study and enjoy its treasures.

In addition to the estate, Huntington's contributions to the country still exist. His railroads helped connect an expanding country. Public parks, beaches, and roads throughout Southern California owe their existence to his ingenuity, and the city of Huntington Beach bears his name. He gave generously to hospitals, churches, schools, including the University of Southern California and the College of William and Mary, and other institutions. Henry Huntington's legacy attests to his devotion to thoroughness; he ensured that the projects completed in his lifetime continue today through their preservation.

# Springtime

Jennie Buteyn

When springtime slowly wakens
In country woodlands fair,
I hear the rustle of the breeze
And smell spring in the air.

The songbirds sweetly sing a song
In the early morning hours.
The sunshine warms the cold, cold soil
To sprout the woodland flowers.

The fleecy clouds in the clear blue sky
And the whippoorwill in the treetop high
Proclaim the Maker's loving care
To all His creatures everywhere.

Photo Opposite
CRABAPPLE PATHWAY
Kennett Square, Pennsylvania
Jane Grushow
Grant Heilman Photography

# A Springtime Prayer

Margaret Rorke

Oh, Lord of Spring in soil and air,
Grant me a life more full and fair
    By putting springtime there.

Grant me a mind that opens up
Like petals of the buttercup
    To see, to sense, to sup.

In me put power to push and grow
Unhampered by the cold and snow,
    Past winter's wind and woe.

Give me a heart by spring renewed
And fed till fertile with the food
    Of love and gratitude.

Implant my soul with strength of seed
That works with wisdom 'gainst the weed
    To fill some human need.

Please oil my every spoken word
With what you use to "song" the bird
    So I'll be sweeter heard.

Oh, Lord, to balance what is rife
With self-concern and senseless strife,
    Put springtime in my life.

# Readers' Forum

Years ago my family received *Ideals* for a gift at Christmas and Easter from my mother. We always enjoyed it. Last year, I bought the Christmas issue for my grandchildren and then subscribed for the year. How glad I am! We spent Easter in Florida with my father, and I just now got the time to read the Easter 1992 issue from "cover to cover." To my joy, I read "Mama's Easter Bonnet" by Beatrice Wheeler Baier. I gave that piece as a recitation in the Christian church in Winner, South Dakota, at least fifty years ago. I often remembered parts of the poem, but I didn't know the author and really didn't take the time to research; but I will keep this special *Ideals* and share it with my children and grandchildren. Thank you for bringing me a memory from my childhood.

Dolores Wendorf
Cass Lake, Minnesota

Since my childhood I have enjoyed *Ideals* and have known it to be an important part of my celebration of the holidays and of the seasons of the year, but I never really realized this until recently. You see, I am a seminarian studying Theology in Rome, Italy, and Rome is a great distance from my home in Pennsylvania. . . . There certainly are many interesting and wonderful things that I have encountered since I have been living in Europe as a student . . . but as I was forewarned, there did come to pass times of deep and heartfelt homesickness. It was during those times, especially around the holidays, that I would reflect upon those same times back home. One of the most special parts of the holidays that I was so happy to recall was the annual bringing out of the *Ideals* with their colorful pictures and illustrations, beautiful poetry, and especially meaningful to me, the moving religious themes which I know somehow played a part in the vocation to the ordained ministry which I am pursuing today. My family sends me *Ideals* here in Rome now, and pausing from my busy schedule to look at each new issue is like sitting down with an old friend that has come to visit.

Paul R. Wolensky
Rome, Italy

Since I spend most of my time in my home, my husband decided to plant a garden for me in my back yard where I could view it from my kitchen window. I took a picture of him while he was working. As I watched him working so hard, I was moved to write the poem that I enclosed, "My Husband Planted a Garden."

Martha Cummins Fischer
Baltimore, Maryland

My husband planted a garden for me
To view from my kitchen window.
A winding, beautiful sight to see
Crepe myrtle, viola, and willow.

Azaleas in spring, mums in the fall,
A gift for all seasons
Where birds come to call.

I look out of my window
Knowing that he
Planted a garden of love for me.